The Most Dangerous Place to Be...

In The Middle of the Road!

by
Roberts Liardon

Unless otherwise indicated, all Scripture quotations are taken from the *King James Version* of the Bible.

Some quotations are taken from the *New King James Version* of the Bible. Copyright © 1979, 1980, 1982, by Thomas Nelson Inc., publishers.

2nd Printing

The Most Dangerous Place to Be...
In the Middle of the Road
ISBN 1-890900-10-9

Copyright © 1999 by Roberts Liardon Ministries.
P.O. Box 30710
Laguna Hills, CA 92654

Published by Embassy Publishing Co.
P.O. Box 3500
Laguna Hills, CA 92654

Printed in the United States of America. All rights reserved under International Copyright Law. Contents and/or cover may not be reproduced in whole or in part in any form without the express written consent of the Publisher.

Contents

1 Jonathan's Tragic End 5

2 Jonathan's Four Chains 11

3 Two Things God Won't Share 17

4 Jonathan's Wrong Loyalties 21

5 It's Your Choice 25

1
Jonathan's Tragic End

Throughout your life you'll have thousands of acquaintances, but not many true friends. You'll be able to count the number of true friends on one hand, probably.

True friends remain faithful during the cloudy days as well as during the sunshine. They stick with you through the thick and thin. They'll be with you in the mud and on the mountain top. Outside of the love of a husband and wife, the love of a true friend is probably one of the deepest loves a person can have. Everyone needs these kinds of friendships in their life. The problem is that they're hard to find and hard to hold on to.

David had a friend like that — his name was Jonathan. I like Jonathan. He is one of my Bible heroes. I've prayed for God to give me Jonathan-type friends in my life because Jonathan was a loyal friend. But the friendship that began so wonderfully between Jonathan and David, later came to a terrible end. It ended with Jonathan dying on a battlefield beside the wicked man who tried to kill his best friend.

Seeds Of True Friendship

In 1 Samuel 18:1 we read about the beginning of David and Jonathan's friendship:

...when he (David) had finished speaking to Saul, the soul of Jonathan was knit to the soul of David, and Jonathan loved him as his own soul. Saul took him that day, and would not let him go home to his father's house anymore. Then Jonathan and David made a covenant, because he loved him as his own soul. And Jonathan took off the robe that was on him and gave it to David, with his armor, even to his sword and his bow and his belt.

1 Sam 18:1-4 (NKJ)

Jonathan was a good friend to have. He had position, honor and wealth. He had access to information and to the presence of great people. His father Saul was the first king of Israel. Jonathan knew how much money Saul had because he was in on all of his father's private conversations. Jonathan stood beside his father through everything.

But Jonathan also knew the facts about his father. He knew Saul's motives. He had watched his father go down to the witch of Endor to inquire of demons. He had watched his father throw a javelin to kill David, his closest companion. Jonathan knew the facts, yet sadly, he chose to die on a battlefield with this backslidden, God-forsaken king.

Did Jonathan have a wicked heart like his father? No. It was obvious he didn't because he protected David from Saul. Jonathan brought the secrets of the chamber talk to David, to warn him to run, because Jonathan knew God had chosen David to be the next great king of Israel. Jonathan was a loyal friend. But he also had a problem; he was loyal to the wrong cause. He knew that God's presence had left Saul's house and yet Jonathan refused to leave the house of error to dwell in the house of righteousness.

The Jonathans Of Today

There are "Jonathans" in churches all over the world today. In fact, some of you reading this book may be Jonathans. You know that God has released a fresh anointing in the earth. You know that God has given His blessing to certain ministries, yet you continue to remain loyal to those who are no longer loyal to God.

Some of you live in places where it is not hard to see where God is at. If you're spiritually discerning, you can see God's hand of blessing on certain ministries. But you can also see the ministries that are built on the movement of man's soul, apart from the blessing of God.

Many of the preachers that once embraced the nine gifts of the Spirit, God's healing miraculous power, God's delivering hand, and the Lord's second coming, are now preaching the opposite. They shun the truth, and the crowd amens it. Many who once interceded to cause the kingdom of God to progress, have joined the ranks of those who live a life of compromise. They attend churches where these things are shunned, made fun of, and disdained. They sit in their chair, give their money and the blessing of their presence, and think that they are in the perfect will of God. Though they don't know it, they are modern-day Jonathans on their way to death on the wrong battlefield.

God is calling His people to make a change from the house of carnality, death, willful error and sin, to the house of those who truly love God and live right before Him.

Jonathan's Tragic End

In 1st Samuel 31:1-6 we read the story of Jonathan's violent death:

Now the Philistines fought against Israel; and the men of Israel fled from before the Philistines, and fell slain on Mount Gilboa. Then the Philistines followed hard after Saul and his sons. And the Philistines killed

Jonathan's Tragic End

Jonathan, Abinadab, and Malchishua, Saul's sons. The battle became fierce against Saul. The archers hit him, and he was severely wounded by the archers. Then Saul said to his armorbearer, "Draw your sword, and thrust me through with it, lest these uncircumcised men come and thrust me through and abuse me." But his armorbearer would not, for he was greatly afraid. Therefore Saul took a sword and fell on it. And when his armorbearer saw that Saul was dead, he also fell on his sword, and died with him. So Saul, his three sons, his armorbearer, and all his men died together that same day.

1 Sam 31:1-6 (NKJ)

After killing Saul and his sons, the Philistines took their bodies and nailed them to the city wall for the birds of the air to pick at their flesh. That is not a rightful way for any man of God to die. They hung them there in sad disgrace, making a mockery of God and the people of Israel — *and Jonathan was with them.* What a tragic end! But it was Jonathan's fault because Jonathan knew what was right and he didn't make the choice to depart from the house of Saul to join with the house of David.

Jonathan represents the person who has a right heart, who knows the truth and is sympathetic toward it, but doesn't have the backbone to make a stand for what is right. What happened to Jonathan was of his own doing. He died fighting for a king who inquired of a witch and made a mockery of God.

How many Jonathans are there in the United States of America? How many Jonathans are there around the world who know the truth, but will not take a stand and move toward what is right? You can know the truth and still die because you don't act upon it. (James 1:22) You can know that it's God's will to heal but be among those who don't believe it and die because of it. You can know that God wants to prosper you, but be among the ones who don't believe it, and you can die broke. That was the sad testimony of Jonathan.

2

Jonathan's Four Chains: Family, Comfort, Privilege & Status

Why was Jonathan so skittish? Why didn't he make the choice to leave the house of Saul and dwell in the house of David? The first reason was that Saul was family. Jonathan would have had to face his father and say, "Dad, I love you, I'll always be your son and I respect you, but I do not support what you're doing. Because of your own willful mistakes, you're trying to murder the man whom God has chosen and anointed. I will not be a part of that."

Blood or not, God's principles do not change. Truth is still truth and right is still right. The reason we have families today who continue in a ditch of continual despair, is because somebody in that family will not stand up and say, "It doesn't matter if my blood is your blood — right is right and wrong is wrong, and I choose to stand for what is right!"

Christians need to stand up against the wrong in their families so they can leave a good inheritance to their children and grandchildren. Jonathan could have given a different history to the house of Saul. It could have been written that Saul acted wickedly, but Jonathan did what was right in the sight of the Lord. That could have been Jonathan's testimony.

Jonathan knew the truth — that's why he was out there helping David. But Jonathan didn't have a backbone to stand up for what was right, and it became his undoing.

The reason there is continual sin and error in certain camps is because we have so many Jonathans. Very few have the guts enough to face the truth and embrace it, no matter who reacts to it.

Family Soul Ties

I was holding a revival meeting in North Carolina where all my family is from, and I had reserved the first two rows for my relatives. Usually, when I come to town, my aunts, uncles and cousins come out to hear me preach. During this particular meeting I had both rows filled with my relatives.

Jonathan's Four Chains

As I preached that evening, something arose in my heart and I found myself saying to them, "I love you all, but I don't love you enough to disobey God for you! I don't love you enough to disobey the heavenly call for you!"

I love my family — all of them — and I take care of them the best I can. But I will never disobey God for them. Never. And you shouldn't either. If all your family members decided to jump off a bridge into a canyon with a raging river, would you jump with them? Of course not. We often make statements like that to our kids about their ungodly friends, but that same principle applies to our families.

Peace-Keepers Vs. Peace-Makers

I'm not trying to provoke a family war, but you're probably already in one. Many Christians are too scared to stand up for what is right because they're afraid their relatives will bark. Most Christians want to be peace-keepers and not peace-makers, and there is a vast difference. A peace-keeper is a Bill Clinton, a peace-maker is a Ronald Reagan. A peace keeper is a John Major of Britain, a peace-maker is a Margret Thatcher. A peace-keeper will do anything to achieve peace. They will even disobey God's principles and change God's standards to do it. But a peace-maker will make peace by standing up for God's principles, even when others react negatively.

Some Christians think they are a peace-makers, when they are really just peace-keepers. They don't stand up for God and make decisions to do things His way because of fear of a family member's reaction. That's why there's not real peace in their family. It's a false peace because they aren't free to express their faith in God while they're around their family.

Comfort

The second reason Jonathan didn't stand up for what was right was because he was addicted to the comforts of Saul's house.

Why do we have Jonathans today in the pulpits of America? Why do we have Jonathans today in the pew of professionally dead churches? Why? Because of fleshly comfort. It's comfortable for their flesh, their rebellious children or their carnal husband or wife. It is comfortable to be in a house that does not fully teach the principles of God's Word. It's comfortable to be in a house that does not speak or deal with their fleshly attitudes.

The greatest problem I have in my own church as we grow, is not the sinner, the ex-prostitute, the drug addict or the punker, it is the California Christian who lives by the dictates of their comfortable flesh and tries to dictate to the atmosphere of my pulpit and my church. I have not had one drunkard say, "I don't like the way you speak in tongues!" They all say, "Can I do that?" But not the Jonathans of California who rotate through my church.

I'm not going to let my family and my church family be named among Saul's house. They will have to make a choice to leave Saul's house and not let their desire for fleshly comfort dictate their thoughts and actions.

Privilege And Status

Why are so many Christians happy to live in a Saul's house today? Because they've got privilege and status. They have people waiting on them hand and foot and they don't have to worry about going out to work in the harvest fields of the earth. They can just sit back and enjoy their life of privilege.

Some have a title in their church and they have a position that gives them a little respect. If you go to church because of a title, my friend, you are a hypocrite! If you're a member of a church because of privilege or position, you've already received your eternal reward!

Please have the heart of Jonathan, but have guts to cross over into the house of David and become a humble worker. Jonathan loved David and he wanted to be in the house of David, but he wouldn't join the house of David. Why? Because of comfort, privilege and status!

Jonathan walked with the king every place he went and he had security guards. His every little whimper was met. He could date whoever he wanted because he was the king's son. He had the privilege of picking the fairest of all. He had a glorious swimming pool where he and his father could swim and talk about the strategies of the kingdom.

A Stern Warning

Jonathan! Jonathan! You're living a lie! Jonathan, we appreciate your good heart, but you're eventually going to die in the house of Saul because of the weakness you're not facing in your life! Jonathan, please wake up before it's too late! Please wake up before you enter a battle that's your last!

Jonathan went to battle with a king who didn't have the favor of God. That's why the slaughter was so great and his martyrdom was so disgraceful.

Jonathans all over the world are attending the churches of Saul's house because they have a business card that says "Elder" or "Deliverance Minister." They like their titles and they don't want to give them up to follow God. May they wake up quickly and join with the house of David before it's too late!

3

Two Things God Will Not Share

There are two things that God will not share with people; glory and vengeance. There have been times in my life when I've felt that someone deserved the ministry of a 2x4! We've all had that emotion before. I confess, I've had that emotion quite often, and I've had to repent of it too. But remember God said, *"Vengeance is mine, says the Lord, I will repay."* (Rom 12:19) God executes vengeance correctly and we don't. We execute vengeance from the emotion and He does it from eternal principle. God will not share His vengeance with anyone.

The other thing that God will not share is His glory. All glory, honor and praise belongs to Him.

The Nun Who Got Free

When I lived in Minnesota, I had an ex-nun work for me. To this day I still can't figure out how a nun became my personal secretary, but she did. And she is a great lady.

One morning during our staff prayer meeting, the Spirit of God showed up in a special way and began blessing her. When we were finished praying, God was still blessing her, so we just left her alone with the Lord. When she came out later, she said, "The Lord told me that He's going to use me." She had been praying for the Lord to use her all morning.

About three months later she came into my office with tears in her eyes.

"I feel so used and abused," she said.

"Well, I haven't abused you. I'm a nice boss, you told me so last week." I responded.

At first I took it personal, but then I thought, "I treat her well and any time she needs a day off I give it to her."

"I just feel so used and abused," she said again.

I didn't have any idea what she was talking about so I just sat at my desk wondering how to respond. Then, suddenly, the Lord said, "Tell her she got exactly what she asked. She asked to be used, so now she's being used." When I spoke that word to my secretary, God blessed her and He did a great work in her.

Two Things God Will Not Share

The Praise Of God
Vs. The Praise Of Man

When people feel used and abused, one of the reasons is because they have a glory problem — they want some of the public accolade for themselves. When they don't get it, they often feel used and abused.

But there is a place where the Christian should glory. They should glory in the fact that the Lord has chosen to use them. (1 Cor 1:31)

Your security, affirmation and sense of significance comes when you realize that, out of all the people in the earth, He chose you to do that particular task. That's where you get the motivation to continue. That's where you feel wonderfully fulfilled and it doesn't matter if anyone pats you on the back and says, "good job." We should be happy and glow because God uses us, not because people praise us. All the accolades belong to Jesus.

So when someone says, "I don't get enough appreciation," it is probably because they have a glory problem. They're trying to take what belongs to God for themselves, and if I remember Biblical history right, Lucifer tried that, and that's how he became the devil. Before, Lucifer was a good name like Michael and Gabriel, but when he tried to take some of the glory – he fell like lightning! God doesn't share His glory or vengeance with anyone.

The Most Dangerous Place to Be

It's very possible that Jonathan had a glory problem. Maybe that's why he wouldn't leave the house of Saul. It could be that he liked the praises of men more than the praises of God.

I thank God He chose me to do what I'm doing. You should be happy that God chose you to do whatever you're doing. Forget about receiving the praises of men and enjoy the way God is using you. That's so important. If you'll learn to think like that, you won't have a glory problem.

4

Jonathan's Wrong Loyalties

Jonathan died for the wrong house. He died for the wrong cause because he had wrong loyalties. He knew the facts about Saul's wickedness and yet he still remained loyal to the house of Saul and died because of it.

God does not require you to be loyal to what is wrong. There are many today who are loyal to the wrong thing. I tell my students, "Your loyalty is appreciated in my church and in my staff, but don't be loyal to me if I preach heresy or live a life of willful sin."

God does not require you to follow a man that lives in consistent and willful wrong. Sometimes ministers preach a degree of loyalty that is not Biblical. Folks, you're not to be loyal to any minister that sleeps around, misuses your money or preaches error.

Some preachers say, "If you leave this church you'll be cursed." I don't understand why, but people fall for that line all the time. Would somebody read the Book? Would somebody please talk to the Author? That's called wrong loyalty!

Jonathan Could Have Joined David

Jonathan could have been respectful to his blood line and still made a choice to be in David's house. Saul would not have understood and he may have even tried to kill Jonathan. But Jonathan could have made that choice and God would have honored and protected him.

Lots of people come to David's house and get blessed. They give their money to help David obey God and they get real happy about it. But then they go back to Saul's house and they wonder why death and destruction is over their life. They're not stupid or blind, they know exactly what they're doing. They know exactly where the Word is being taught correctly. They know exactly where the spiritual water is for them to drink. They know exactly where the power is to get their child healed and off of drugs, but because of wrong loyalties, they won't make a choice to leave the house of Saul and join the house of David.

Jonathan Was Probably Convicted

I'll guarantee you that Jonathan had a raging battle within himself. I'm sure he thought, "I love David. The anointing is on David and what he's telling me is right.

Jonathan's Wrong Loyalties

I love my father too, but God has withdrawn His anointing from him. My father has committed willful sins and has not repented. And when he does repent, it's only for a moment of public prestige — it's not from the heart." I am sure that the war raged within Jonathan day and night, but he never had enough guts to cross the line and join with David. How sad.

That's where many are at in the Body of Christ today. There are Jonathans all over the world that must make a decision. What house are you going to align yourself with?

5
It's Your Choice

Some of you reading this book attend a church that doesn't believe in God's power to deliver, heal and prosper. They may say they do, but you can tell that they really don't because they don't have much of it in operation. Don't die in the house of Saul! Cross over and be a part of the house of David before its too late!

You can't live by a corporate decision, you have to make your own decisions. You can't walk into David's house because this book has influenced you. You've got to make the decision to leave Saul's house for yourself. Hopefully this message has challenged you enough to evaluate what kind of house you're in and make a choice. God is looking for action and not just talk. He is waiting for you to stand up and do what is right.

As we begin the new millennium, many Jonathans around the world will cross the line and join the house of David!

The House Of Saul
Vs. The House Of David

I've made a list of three things comparing the house of Saul to the house of David. Let me just give them to you in closing.

1) Saul was a selfish king. The great prophet Samuel warned the people that as soon as they chose a king, he would take to himself their sons and daughters, their gold and the best of their wheat for himself. (1 Sam 8:11-18) David, on other hand, served his own generation by doing the will of God. (Acts 13:36) David's heart was towards God as well as toward his generation.

2) When Saul sinned, he made excuses, but when David sinned, he repented. Saul offered the priest's sacrifice and did what was not his right to do. This is a type and a shadow of a man assuming a ministry position that was not given to him. So the prophet Samuel came and said, "Hey, what's the lowing of the oxen, and the bleating of the sheep that I hear?"

Saul didn't repent. He said, "Well I did it for the people — the people made me do it."

Excuses. Excuses. Excuses.

When David committed adultery with Bathsheba and he became a murderer and a liar, he didn't blame Bathsheba. He repented and said, "I have sinned." He changed his ways and took the judgment of his actions. You can follow a man like that.

Men sin and make mistakes. Men make errors, but if they say, "I have sinned," and then get it right, you can keep following them.

Saul didn't do that, he just made excuses. I can stand behind a man that has done wrong and repents. But a man who makes excuses is going to go down with the ship.

3)   David worked correctly with the priests and the prophets and he obeyed their words, but Saul killed many of God's priests because he didn't like them. Saul went to the witch of Endor for counsel but David obeyed the prophets.

Jonathan, Move Before It's Too Late!

Jonathan knew the facts about Saul. Folks, you know the facts, too. Are you in the right house spiritually? Are you scared to be seen in the house of David? Are you afraid that it might upset your religious status? Maybe that's why you bought this book. You're too scared to come over to the house of David, so you buy David's books and tapes because you know what he's saying is right! Hey, Jonathan! Are you going to die on the wrong battlefield? It's your choice!

I can hear many saying, "But Roberts, you don't understand!"

The Most Dangerous Place to Be

I don't want to understand! I don't want the ability to somehow agree with your decision to die in the house of Saul!

Many Christians attend churches that say they believe in the fullness of God's Word and the power of the Holy Spirit, but they never allow it, propagate it, or walk in it. Many Christians go to a house where carnality rules, but it doesn't bother them because they have status, comfort and privilege. Yes, they may feel good for a moment and look great for ten years, but they will ultimately die for a worthless cause.

I don't understand why anyone would want to stay in a seeker-friendly church when they could go to one that imparts the fullness of God's power and strength into their life!

There was no honor in the death of Jonathan. There was no respect in his death. Everybody knew that the house of Saul was going have a tragic end because the writing was on the wall. It had been written there by the actions of Saul.

Some people try to play a game. I guess they like to gamble. I guess they like to see how long can they can stay before it bites them. If you no longer see things in the absolutes of right and wrong, then you've been already been bitten!

Don't lose your inner conviction! Don't lose that stronghold of truth that is within you! Don't lose that inward part that reacts to compromise! The middle of the road is a dangerous place to be! Get up and say, "I love you Saul, but I don't agree with what you're doing! I will not continue with you in this! I will not die with you for this! I'm getting up and I'm taking my whole family over to the house of David. Good-bye."

Notes

Notes

Notes

Notes

BOOKS
by Roberts Liardon

A Call To Action

Cry Of The Spirit

Extremists, Radicals and Non-Conformists

Final Approach

Forget Not His Benefits

God's Generals

Haunted Houses, Ghosts, And Demons

Holding To The Word of The Lord

I Saw Heaven

Kathryn Kuhlman

Knowing People By The Spirit

On Her Knees

Religious Politics

Run To The Battle

School of The Spirit

Sharpening Your Discernment

Smith Wigglesworth - Complete Collection

Smith Wigglesworth Speaks To Students

Spiritual Timing

The Invading Force

The Most Dangerous Place To Be

The Price of Spiritual Power

The Quest For Spiritual Hunger

Three Outs and You're In

To place an order call (949) 833-3555
or visit our website at: www.robertsliardon.org

Spirit Life Partner

Wouldn't It Be Great...

- If you could feed over 1,000 hungry people every week?
- If you could travel 250,000 air miles, boldly preaching the Word of God in 93 nations?
- If you could strengthen and train the next generation of God's leaders?
- If you could translate 23 books and distribute them into 37 countries?

Project Joseph Food Outreach.

...Now You Can!

Maybe you can't go, but by supporting this ministry every month, your gift can help to communicate the gospel around the world.

CLIP ALONG LINE & MAIL TO ROBERTS LIARDON MINISTRIES.

☐ **YES!!** Pastor Roberts, I want to support your work in the kingdom of God by becoming a **SPIRIT LIFE PARTNER**. Please find enclosed my first monthly gift.

Name _____
Address _____
City _____ State _____ Zip _____
Phone (_____) _____
SPIRIT LIFE PARTNER AMOUNT: $ _____
☐ Check / Money Order ☐ VISA ☐ American Express ☐ Discover ☐ MasterCard

☐☐☐☐ ☐☐☐☐ ☐☐☐☐ ☐☐☐☐

Name On Card _____ Exp. Date ___/___

Signature _____ Date ___/___

Roberts Liardon Ministries
P.O. Box 30710 ♦ Laguna Hills, CA 92654 ♦ (949) 833-3555 ♦ Fax (949) 833.9555 ♦ www.robertsliardon.org

AUDIO TAPES *by Roberts Liardon*

Acts of The Holy Spirit
Be Strong In The Lord
Breaking the Cycle of Failure
Changing Spiritual Climates
God's Secret Agents
Haunted Houses, Ghosts, & Demons
How To Combat Demonic Forces
How To Stay On The Mountaintop
How To Stir Up Your Calling
    and Walk In Your Gifts
How To Survive An Attack
Increasing Your Spiritual Capacity
I Saw Heaven
Life & Ministry of Kathryn Kuhlman
Living On The Offensive
No More Religion
Obtaining Your Financial Harvest
Occupy 'Til He Comes
Personality of the Holy Spirit
Prayer 1 - How I Learned To Pray
Prayer 2 - Lost In The Spirit
Reformers & Revivalists
Rivers of Living Water (Grams)
School of The Spirit
Seven Steps of Demonic Posession
Sharpening Your Discernment (One)
Sharpening Your Discernment (Two)
Spirit Life
Spiritual Climates
Storms of His Presence
Taking A City
Tired? How To Live In The
    Divine Life of God
True Spiritual Strength
The Anointing
The Healing Evangelists
The Charges of St. Paul - 1 Timothy
The Charges of St. Paul - 2 Timothy
The Working of Miracles
    & Divine Health
Three Arenas of Authority
    & Conflict
Three Worlds: God, You,
    & The Devil
Tired? How To Live In The
    Divine Life Of God
Tongues And Their Diversities
True Spiritual Strength
Useable Faith
Victorious Living In The Last Days
Working The Word
What You Need To Keep
    Under To Go Over
Your Faith Stops The Devil

To place an order call (949) 833-3555
or visit our website at: www.robertsliardon.org

Seven reasons you should attend Spirit Life Bible College

1. SLBC is a **spiritual school** with an academic support; not an academic school with a spiritual touch.

2. SLBC teachers are **successful ministers** in their own right. Pastor Roberts Liardon will not allow failure to be imparted into his students.

3. SLBC is a member of **Oral Roberts University Educational Fellowship** and is **fully accredited** by the International Christian Accreditation Association.

4. SLBC hosts monthly seminars with some of the **world's greatest** ministers who add another element, anointing and impartation to the students' lives.

5. Roberts Liardon understands your commitment to come to SLBC and commits himself to students by **ministering weekly** in classroom settings.

6. SLBC provides **hands-on** ministerial training.

7. SLBC provides ministry opportunity through its **post-graduate placement program**.

CLIP ALONG LINE & MAIL TO ROBERTS LIARDON MINISTRIES.

☐ **YES!!** Pastor Roberts, I am interested in attending **SPIRIT LIFE BIBLE COLLEGE**. Please send me an information packet.

Name _____

Address _____

City _____ State _____ Zip _____

Phone (_____) _____

Roberts Liardon Ministries
P.O. Box 30710 ♦ Laguna Hills, CA 92654
(949) 833-3555 ♦ Fax (949) 833.9555
www.robertsliardon.org

We do not discriminate regardless of race, color, national origin, sex, or age.

VIDEO TAPES *by Roberts Liardon*

2+2=4
And The Cloud Came
A New Generation
Apostles, Prophets
    & Territorial Churches
Apostolic Alignment
Are You A Prophet?
Confronting The Brazen Heavens
Developing An Excellent Spirit
Don't Break Rank
Does Your Pastor Carry A Knife?
Forget Not His Benefits
God's Explosive Weapons
How To Be An End Time Servant
How To Be Healed
    of Spiritual Blindness
I Saw Heaven
Ministering To The Lord
No More Walls
Reformers And Revivalists (5 Vol.)
Spirit of Evangelism
The Importance of Praying
    In Tongues
The Lord Is A Warrior
The Most Dangerous Place To Be
The New Millennium Roar
The Operation of Exhortation
The Word of The Lord Came
    Unto Me Saying
True And False Manifestations

Was Jesus Religious?
Why God Wrote Verse 28

New God's Generals Video Collection

Volume 1 - John Alexander Dowie
Volume 2 - Maria Woodworth-Etter
Volume 3 - Evan Roberts
Volume 4 - Charles F. Parham &
    William J. Seymour
Volume 5 - John G. Lake
Volume 6 - Smith Wigglesworth
Volume 7 - Aimee Semple
    McPherson
Volume 8 - William Branham
Volume 9 - Jack Coe
Volume 10 - A. A. Allen
Volume 11 - Kathryn Kuhlman
Volume 12 - Highlights
    & Live Footage

Videos by Gladoylene Moore (Grams)

Foundations of Stone
God of the Breakthrough
How I Learned To Pray
How To Avoid Disaster
Seeking God
The Prophetic Flow
The Sword Of Gideon
The Warrior Names of God

*To place an order call (949) 833-3555
or visit our website at: www.robertsliardon.org*

ROBERTS LIARDON MINISTRIES INTERNATIONAL OFFICES

EUROPE
Roberts Liardon Ministries
P.O. Box 2043
Hove, Brighton
East Sussex, BN3 6JU
England
011-44-1707-327-222

SOUTH AFRICA
Roberts Liardon Ministries
P.O. Box 3155
Kimberly 8300
South Africa
011-27-53-832-1207

AUSTRALIA
Roberts Liardon Ministries
P.O. Box 7
Kingsgrove, NSW
1480
Australia
011-61-500-555-056

Roberts Liardon Ministries
P.O. Box 30710
Laguna Hills, California, USA
92654-0710
Telephone: (949) 833-3555
Fax: (949) 833-9555
Visit our website at: www.robertsliardon.org